ABANDONED

A DeVontray and His Brothers

Series

Book 1

Jamantha Watson

"Call to ME and I will answer you. I'll tell you marvelous and wondrous things that you could never figure out on your own."-

Jeremiah 33:3

About The Author

It was Thursday.

The temperature in Buffalo, New York was frigid that afternoon; as snow fell in heavy clumps; and the class sat warming up after recess. It was the perfect time to write an essay. There, in Ms. Mimm's English class, Jamantha Watson wrote her first short story. "My Family's Camping Adventures" detailed an exciting hiking trip into the Alleghany Mountains. Not only did Watson's English teacher find the story amusing, her classmates did as well. As a result, writing and reading about her parents and siblings peaked an interest in storytelling.

Because her parents had instilled the importance of both writing and reading and the incredible nourishment they both added to an individual's overall development, Watson read voraciously and has since enjoyed devouring gazillions of books. Today, Jamantha Watson encourages youngsters to read books whenever and wherever they can. She believes that making reading a favorite hobby is ideal

to all students, everywhere.

One of the author's hobbies is collecting inspirational quotes.

Her absolute favorite was once written by a man named Dr. Seuss. It

states, "You have brains in your head. You have feet in your shoes.

You can steer yourself any direction you choose."

The author and the publishers at Epaga House Publishing, Inc. wish you and your family a most incredible reading adventure.

For children everywhere

Chapter One

COMING HOME

"Ma," DeVontray called, walking around the empty house searching for his mother. "Hello? Mommy are you in here?" He ran upstairs. She wasn't there. He ran back to the kitchen. She wasn't there either.

Looking around the kitchen, DeVontray wondered what in the world had happened to the other three kitchen chairs. And where, he **wondered**, was the kitchen table? All of the kitchen furniture had been in there **usual** places when he and his brothers had gone off to school earlier that morning. Everything had been in the middle of the kitchen floor, just as it always had been. Months had passed since they'd seen the living room furniture, their television sets, their dressers or their heavy winter coats. But today even the kitchen furniture was gone too. Now that everything was gone, DeVontray knew he and his brothers wouldn't even have a place to sit and do homework nor eat dinner. If there was any dinner.

Dragging the only foot stool in the house from one end of the kitchen to the other, DeVontray slid the stool as close to the cupboard as he could get it. Opening the cupboard door, he grabbed the last bag of noodles he saw. His stomach growled as he slid the stool back across the room, underneath the window. The tick–tocking of the apple shaped clock reminded him that in a couple of hours it would be dark. Already the little hand was on the three. The big hand was inching its way up to the twelve. The clock's ticking also reminded DeVontray that it had been several hours since he'd eaten lunch at school.

At school, all the teachers were excited about possibly having the next day off. If it snowed, like the weatherman said it would, all the schools in the city of Richmond and the surrounding counties would be closed. The good thing about the snow was that he and his younger brothers would be able to go outside and build snowmen, snow castles and angels. The bad part was that neither of them would get anything to eat at home. The two full course meals they had come to rely on five days a week, came from McKinley Elementary School. Lately, breakfast and lunch had become the only **guaranteed** meals in their day.

Closing his eyes, DeVontray prayed for clear weather. Prayed that God would not let the bad snowstorm come any time soon, at least not until their mother had come back home to be with the three of them. If she decided to come back before the storm, they'd all go grocery shopping and be happy again. But, something told him their mother wouldn't be coming home tonight. He couldn't remember the last time he and his little brothers had seen her. Six days? Seven? Two weeks maybe? He'd lost count of the last time they'd seen her walk through their door. Because of the missing kitchen furniture, the feeling in his gut told him his mother had been home today. His gut also told him she would not be coming back home to prepare supper nor to help them with homework.

Pouring a glass of water into the large frying pan, he opened the bag of dried noodles and crushed them into the pan. Whether his mother came home today or not, he knew he had to make sure his two brothers, Keon and Marquis had some food to fill their stomachs before they completed their homework and went to bed. Looking into the refrigerator, DeVontray's heart pounded with excitement when he saw the only thing sitting on the shelf; a hot dog wrapped in plastic. For the past week, the refrigerator had been completely bare.

He smiled knowing that if he cut the hot dog into tiny pieces, his brothers would have more than just noodles for dinner. Perhaps neither of them would have to go to bed crying of a terrible head or stomach ache.

"We're back," he heard Keon say, slamming the front door.

"Yeah," said their baby brother, "we're back."

"Did y'all eat something at Mrs. Trueheart's house?" DeVontray asked. He had always told his brothers to go visit a neighbor's house directly after school and stay long enough to eat at least a snack. The one house they were not to visit was Mr. and Mrs. Green's. According to their mother, the Greens were uppity black folk. They drove nice cars, paid a company to keep their grass green all year round; and had the most beautiful home in the entire neighborhood. And for five years straight, their house had been mentioned in the newspaper as one of the best decorated houses during the Christmas season. Besides, Devontray thought, Mr. and Mrs. Green taught college. They were too busy thinking about reading books, to ever care about feeding someone else. Black folk like that, his mother had told them, always thought they were better than most other black folk. So, she had warned them to stay far, far away.

"Yeah, Mrs. Trueheart fed us," Keon said.

"Good. What did y'all eat?"

"Hot chocolate and ham biscuits."

Marquis scrunched his face. "But they were too salty."

"So what Marquis, you crushed every last one of those salty ham biscuits. I didn't hear you complaining about how salty they were when you were crushing them."

"I never said I was **complaining** about those salty biscuits, back then, Keon. But I'm complaining about them now," he stuck his tongue out at Keon. "So be quiet."

Keon sucked his teeth. "Anyway…," he said, "Mrs. Trueheart said those ham biscuits were from that thing at her church yesterday. Her usher's group had some leftovers and she said she didn't mind sharing them with us." Keon zipped up his coat. "Why is it so cold in here?"

DeVontray looked at his brothers, one in kindergarten, the other in first grade. At nine years old and in the fourth grade, DeVontray was the oldest, but still wasn't much taller nor bigger than either of his siblings. Mrs. Trueheart once told him he was small

framed because he wasn't being 'properly nourished' at home. At the

time he didn't really understand those big words, but he had a feeling

that not being 'properly **nourished**' was not a good thing to be.

When he asked Mrs. Trueheart what she'd meant, she explained

herself to him.

"Not enough vitamins and minerals in your body," she'd told

him. "In order for you to grow strong and healthy, you have to eat

foods that are healthy for you; foods that give you a lot of strength

and make you grow into being a big man."

He patted his growling stomach and tried not to think of food.

With a quick sweep of his eyes, DeVontray once again looked around

the kitchen. Their house was not the biggest house he'd ever been in,

but now that all of their furniture had disappeared, their home seemed

nearly as large as his kindergarten teacher's, Miss Wooten. Even

talking to his brothers sounded different. Speaking to one another

sounded as if they were talking, deep inside Miss Wooten's well;

echoing every time they talked.

"Y'all come on and get ready to eat dinner. That'll warm you up," DeVontray said to his brothers. "All I could find were some noodles and a hotdog for y'all to eat."

"Gross," said Marquis, shaking his head.

"Well at least that's better than us eating that nasty can of spaghetti, mixed with peas and applesauce," Keon responded.

"As long as we get properly nourished," DeVontray remembered Mrs. Trueheart's words. "We gotta grow up to be strong and healthy."

Trying not to burn himself, DeVontray scooped out as many noodles and pieces of hot dogs into two bowls as he could. He didn't bother grabbinng a third bowl for himself. His only concern was feeding his brothers. If they could go without getting hungry, he'd be satisfied. His stomach hurt him so much; he could no longer feel the hunger. Staying busy, thinking of other things helped keep his mind off of food.

"Where are we supposed to sit down to eat?" asked Keon.

"Find a spot somewhere," DeVontray snapped, sounding more like his mother than himself. His eyes followed his baby brother Marquis, as he roamed the kitchen looking for a place to sit.

"Where are we supposed to sit down?" Marquis asked.

"Marquis, I just told Keon to find a spot somewhere!"

Keon chimed in, "But what happened to the kitchen table and the chairs and…?"

"I don't know," DeVontray cut him off, "just sit down somewhere on the floor, please. There's only a stool in the house now. One person can sit on the stairs. One person can sit on the floor and somebody else can take the stool. It really doesn't matter."

Chapter One

Words to Know

Wondered – (verb) to have an interest in knowing or learning something.

Usual – (adjective) done, found, or used most of the time or in most cases: normal or regular

Guaranteed – (verb) to say (something) with great confidence

Complaining- (verb) to say or write that you are unhappy

Nourished – (verb) to provide (someone or something) with food and other things that are needed to live, be healthy

Echoing (verb) –to fill a space, area with sounds

Chapter One
Cross Word Puzzle

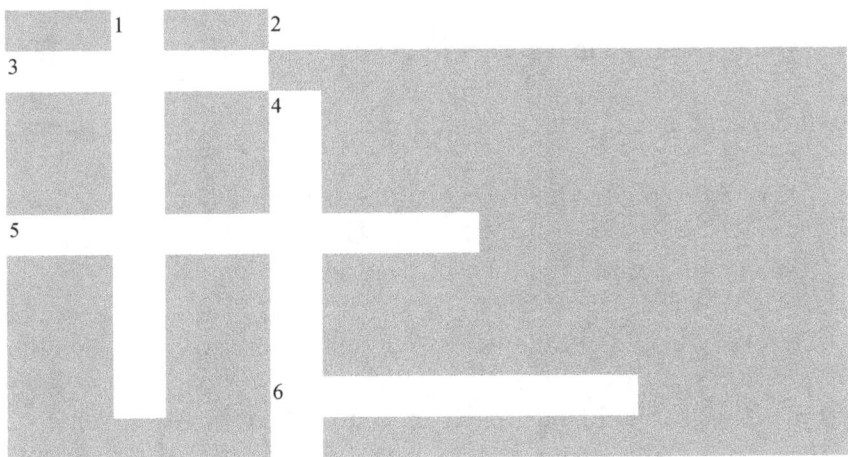

ACROSS

2. to say or write that you are unhappy
3. done, found, or used most of the time or in most cases: normal or regular
5. to have an interest in knowing or learning something
6. to fill a space, area with sounds

DOWN

1. to say (something) with great confidence
4. to provide (someone or something) with food and other things that are needed to live, be healthy

Chapter Two

MR. MOM

Marquis walked to a corner in the kitchen. He sat there with the bowl beside his feet, his knees pulled to his chin. Walking over to him, DeVontray put his hand on his little brother's shoulder.

"What's the matter with you Lil' Man?"

Before he could get the words out, tears were rolling down his chubby cheeks, "I'm cold and I miss mommy," he **whined**. "Why doesn't she come home to us anymore?" The more he wiped his round face, the faster the tears rolled.

Without turning, DeVontray could tell by the soft sniffling behind him that Keon was also crying, although his spoon was **steadily** tapping the bowl. Keon always wanted to seem as if he was so big and bad, but whenever the subject of their mother came up, all three of the boys became sad, even Keon.

"She'll be back soon Lil' Man," DeVontray tried to sound grown up, like an adult. He tried to hold back the tears himself, but when he felt the knot in his throat, he knew the tears would soon be falling.

"But when she does come home," he blinked back the tears, "she wants you to eat up all your food, so you won't get sick, alright?" he sniffled.

Marquis looked up to his big brother and nodded.

DeVontray walked toward the window and leaned against it. He placed his hand over the book of matches and the small glass tube, both resting on the windowsill and quickly shoved them in his back pocket. If his brothers had seen the matches and the tube, they would have probably begun to ask several questions about their mother. And that would just have started them crying all over again. He knew from the two things he'd shoved in his pocket that their mother had been home earlier that day. He also knew that it was time for her to return. DeVontray had to think of a way to try and find her and bring her back home to them.

Looking out the window, he imagined how the teachers at McKinley Elementary School were probably at home with their families smiling as they watched the snow come down in large clumps from the sky. He thought of bread falling from the sky, like that bible story he had heard about in Sunday school class. Man, how he wished bread would fall down from the sky like that right now. Man, how he wished he had prayed harder to God about keeping the snow away.

Pressing his forehead against the window, he could see Jaquan and his sister Nautica get out of the car with their mother and father. Each of them carried a bag of groceries. Neither Jaquan nor Nautica would be going to bed hungry tonight. He wondered what they would eat for dinner. Spaghetti? Hot dogs? Fried chicken? Mashed potatoes? Hamburgers? Sloppy Joes? Pizza?

His stomach got angrier and angrier with him, **growling** back like a beast. Maybe he and his brothers could invite themselves over to Jaquan's house for dinner. Maybe he could go to Mrs. Trueheart's house and tell her that their mother hadn't gotten home yet and all three of them needed to be 'properly nourished.' Maybe then they could get another full course meal before they all went to sleep. But DeVontray remembered how his mother had once told them, no matter how long she was gone; they were not allowed to tell anyone *her* business. And he thought while scratching his head, talking to someone else about his mother's absence from home, was only her business. No one else's.

"You finished?" He looked at his baby brother, who was walking toward him licking the bowl.

Marquis nodded, extending the bowl, "I want some more."

"Ain't no more," Keon shouted, scooping the remains of food out of the bowl with his finger.

"I'll find some more," DeVontray whispered, "I promise."

"Whatever," Keon said, dropping his spoon and bowl into the kitchen sink. "Come on Marquis, let's go outside. It's just as cold in here as it is outside anyway. May as well go out there and have some fun in the snow. May as well."

"Can we go make angels in the snow DeVontray?" Marquis asked sadly.

"Yeah, Lil Man, y'all go on"

DeVontray knew how to cook. He had learned how to **create** many different recipes. He knew if he could find some food to tie them over for the next few days they wouldn't have to be so hungry. But the one thing he didn't want to do was to walk where he knew he had to walk to get it. Besides, it was just too cold outside. Later on tonight, inside their house it would be even colder. And it wasn't just cold inside the house because of the outside temperature. It was cold inside their house because the heat had been turned off by the gas company downtown.

Staring at the white sheet of paper taped to the side of the refrigerator from Wellington Heating and Oil, he knew his mother had smoked all of their heat money. The paper had been taped to the outside of the front door yesterday afternoon when they got off the school bus. But he had taken it off, sticking it to the refrigerator, hoping his mother would have eventually seen the note and done something about it.

DeVontray frowned, knowing he had put the correct amount of money, eighty – seven dollars, in the gas company's envelope. He remembered opening their mailbox and sliding the envelope through so the mailman could take it when he came later that day. The same way his mother explained to him, was the exact same way he had done it. He always did what she told him to do. So why was there still no heat in their house?

If their mother didn't come home soon, the school would find out and they'd all be kicked out of their house and separated into other schools with other families.   The same thing had happened to

Chavonne and her sisters.   More than anything else, having him and

his brothers being split in three different directions was the main

thing that frightened him.   And lately, Ms. Clark had been sending

him to the principal's office.   Both his teacher and the principal

warned him to lose the attitude or he'd have to be **suspended**.

"Too much attitude."

"Too many anger issues."

He was always being too mean to the other students.   Always

too this, always too that.

Today Ms. Clark sent him to the principal's office because he

picked up his desk and threw it against the wall.   The hole the desk

made in the wall was so large, Dorian, the biggest boy in the class,

spread both arms across the hole and still couldn't cover it.

Yesterday DeVontray got sent to the principal's office because he

had gotten so mad at what Ha'asan had said about his mother, that he

banged the front of his own head against the desk, over and over and

over again.   Every day it was something different.   And every day

since his mother was gone, he had caused some kind of commotion in

the classroom.   But that's how everyone else saw him.

No one ever said how well he cooked the meals for his brothers. They never noticed how he had to wake up earlier than everyone else every morning, just to make sure the boys had washed up, brushed their teeth and put on their school uniforms, **correctly**. People never stopped to think that just because he yelled and threw things at school, he never wanted his brothers to see him act out like that at home. They might become afraid of him, like they were of their mother's boyfriend, Smooth.

Chapter Two
Words to Know

Whined - (verb) to complain in an annoying way; a high crying sound

Steadily - (adjective) direct or sure in movement

Growling - (verb) to make a low sound

Create - (verb) to make or produce something by using talents and imagination

Suspended - (verb) to something for a usually short period of time

Correctly – (adjective) agreeing with facts; having no errors or mistakes

Chapter Two

Cross Word Puzzle

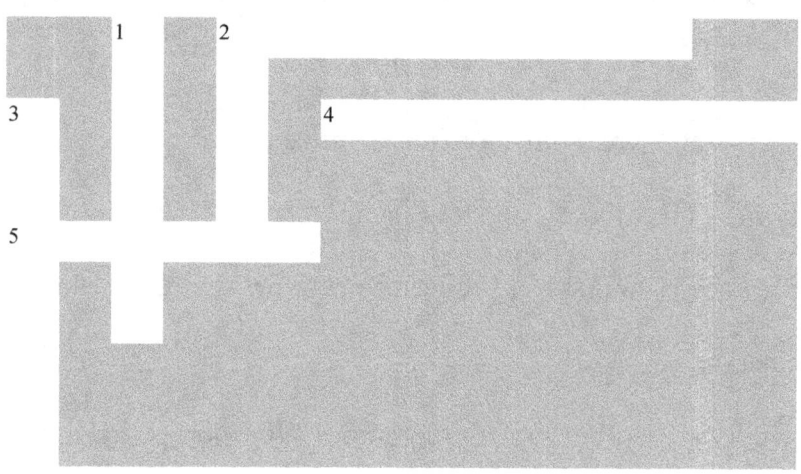

ACROSS

2. agreeing with facts; having no errors or mistakes
4. to something for a usually short period of time
5. to complain in an annoying way; a high crying sound

DOWN

1. direct or sure in movement
2. to make or produce something by using talents and imagination
3. to make a low sound

Chapter Three

FINDING A WAY

OUT

At school, things were different. If he acted out at school, there would be other people to calm him back down. If only his teachers had listened they would know that he just wanted someone to understand him. He wasn't really being mean and angry at anyone in particular. Sometimes, just any little thing would send him into a 'fit of rage' like Ms. Clark often said. But it didn't always have to be anyone else's fault at school. He wasn't mad at anyone at school. The person he was really upset with was his mother. He was angry with her for not coming home to them every day. And he was angry with his mother's boyfriend, Smooth, for spanking them whenever he felt like it. He couldn't pick up his mother and her boyfriend and throw them across the room. But he could pick up his desk. So the only way he knew to fight back at his mother and at her boyfriend was to throw a desk, turn over a table, bang his head against the desk, stomp his feet or pound his fists.

DeVontray really didn't mean any harm to anyone else. He really just wanted to live a normal life again. But all because of his anger he had ended up in a classroom with other special education boys, who were just like him; angry all the time. The LD class, which really meant, Learning Disabled, was where the principal said he belonged. His mother agreed, and that's where he spent every day at school.

Before his mother met Smooth and Smooth's friends, their house was quiet, warm, nice. It had lots of furniture in it too. Their mother worked her job at the post office, came home and cooked delicious hot food for them to eat. That was just last year. This year their mother was pregnant and that really only meant one thing. DeVontray was going to have to find food for one more kid in the house.

Closing his eye, he listened to the laughter of his brothers and the other neighborhood children, making angels in the snow and throwing snowballs. He wondered whether or not the snow would pile up so high tonight he wouldn't be able to walk to get them the food he knew they needed. He wondered if his legs and arms would **cramp** up and hurt again tonight, like they always did when it got so cold in the house. He wondered how different his life would be if he lived with another family, in another house, in another neighborhood. He smiled at the thought. The idea made his body warm all over. In just that instant, he knew what he had to do.

The simple idea of running away really satisfied him more than anything else. If he could run far away from where he was right now, far away into someone else's big, warm cozy house; he would be happier. He could leave his brothers at home. Keon was big and bad enough to start looking around for food for Marquis and himself. Anyway Marquis would soon be in first grade. He would have to learn how to take care of himself too. DeVontray thought hard about the idea of running away. It widened his smile. But thinking of leaving his brothers caused his smile to fade away. Isn't that what their mother kept doing to them? Running away? Every chance she got she ran.

The first time she'd left them was the month after their father's funeral. After their father died, their mother hardly got out of bed to go to church, to go to work, to go anywhere. Before long, she wasn't going to work, because her job had asked her not to come back to them anymore. Not long after she stopped going to work, she met Smooth. Then their Grandma Nanny died and that's when their mother really began running away, leaving DeVontray and his brothers all alone.

He scratched his head, and wondered if going to look for their mother was the same thing as running away. Another idea hit him. Instead of leaving, he could always go work for Big Red. Big Red was a very tall man who **frightened** mostly everyone in their neighborhood. When they were old enough, some of the boys in their community went to work for him, doing things they didn't always want to do. Just last week, Big Red had told DeVontray to leave their house and come stay with him.

"No thanks. I'll take care of me and my brothers by myself," he said, believing every word.

When their mother first began **disappearing**, it was Big Red who would stop in and check on DeVontray and his brothers. It was also Big Red who would bring large buckets of fried chicken, biscuits and cold slaw for them when they were starving. Lately Big Red had stopped bringing food by. One of the neighbors said he had gotten locked up. DeVontray knew that pretty soon when Big Red got out, one of his main priorities would be for DeVontray to come work for him. And although he knew he and his brothers would stay warm and well fed if they went to go live with Big Red; his gut told him that working for that man may not have been the best thing to do. Shrugging his shoulders, he closed his eyes and prayed.

Later that night all three boys lay on the kitchen floor. Their thin jackets and **scraggly** caps adding an extra layer of heat the bed covers they'd placed on the floor could not. DeVontray rubbed his stiff arms and legs and remembered the word his mother had used to describe the pain in his aching body.

Arthritis.

Whenever the heat had gotten turned off and he'd gotten too cold, he'd feel his legs and arms get stiffer until he was barely able to move them at all.

Sitting up, he looked at his snoring brothers. He took the blanket off his body and spread it across Marquis and Keon. His pillow, he placed between their two heads. Before opening the front door, DeVontray walked back to his brothers. He thought of getting his composition book from his backpack and writing them a letter. He'd seen people do it on television many times before. But, on television, children wrote runaway letters to their parents, not to their little brothers. Shooing away the letter idea, DeVontray walked toward the door and opened it.

Maybe he should at least explain why he couldn't hang around anymore. Maybe by him running away, his teachers would take him out of that special education classroom and put him back in the other classroom with all his friends he'd known since Head Start. God knows he had prayed that would happen.

DeVontray didn't want to **disturb** his brothers by rustling papers nor by walking too hard on the floor, so he very quietly sat on the floor beside them, using the moonlight to write his letter.

Dear: Keon and Marquis,

I have to go find mommy. I will bring her back home soon. Everything will be alright. I promise. Say your prayers.

Love y'all,

DeVontray

He placed the opened composition book on the floor above their pillows. When they woke up, Keon would be able to read the letter to Marquis.

Chapter Three

Words to Know

Cramp – (noun) a painful and stiff muscle

Frightened – (verb) to cause someone to be afraid

Disappearing – (verb) to stop being visible; to go to a place that is not known

Scraggly – (adjective) growing in a way that is not neat and even

Arthritis – (noun) a disease that causes the joints to become swollen and painful

Disturbing – (adjective) causing annoyance

Chapter Three

Crossword Puzzle

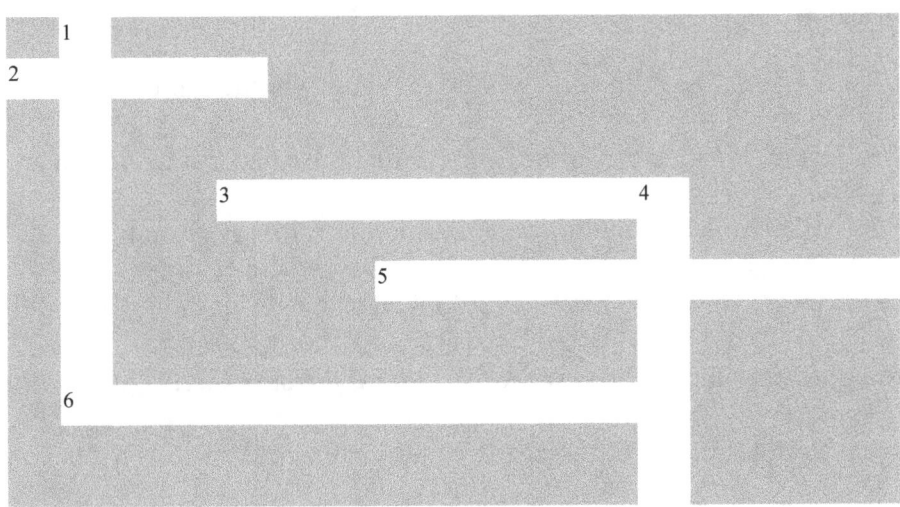

ACROSS

2. a painful and stiff muscle
3. a disease that causes the joints to become swollen and painful
5. causing annoyance
6. to stop being visible; to go to a place that is not known

DOWN

1. to cause someone to be afraid
4. growing in a way that is not neat and even

Chapter Four

A MOUTHFUL

Even though the cold windy night air whipped through his thin jacket, the idea of walking out of the house and not having to think of anyone else but himself, warmed DeVontray from his head to his toes. Snow had never, ever looked as beautiful to him as it did tonight. And the way the snow fell around the street lights, made it seem as if he was walking into a whole new world. That's right DeVontray thought. A whole new world! Tonight I'm starting over in a new world. A new house, a new mother, new food. And one day my new family and I will come back to get my brothers, and we'll all live happily ever after.

Other than to find food, DeVontray had no idea where he was going. He had no clue when this new world would pop out at him. He believed however, if he just kept putting one foot in front of the other foot, he'd find his new world. He thought of Mrs. Trueheart and his Sunday school teacher. He thought on how they, just like

Rev. Blanton had told the children at church to always trust in Jesus, because Jesus loved little children everywhere. He knew now, was a very good time to take their **advice**.

The more DeVontray plowed through the ankle deep snow, the happier he became. Still, something deep down inside nudged him to turn back to his brothers, to his home. He knew if he continued walking, he'd be making the same bad choices his mother made. Well…he thought, first I'll just see how being on my own feels, then if I don't like it, I'll go back home. After all, he **convinced** himself, I am trying to find mommy.

Trudging through the snow, he knew he would have to walk much further down the street, then turn right to go get the food he really wanted. The faster he walked the more he slipped, slid, finally falling bottom first, in the snow.

"Ouch."

The snow was coming down faster, but DeVontray continued on until he saw the sign that blinked *Fanelli's Italian Restaurant*. The letters in the sign twinkled red and green. DeVontray walked toward it. As long as he could get a bite of Mr. Fanelli's good food, he didn't mind falling in the snow. The food Mr. Fanelli served at his restaurant was some of the best DeVotray had ever tasted. Already his tongue was watering as he smelled the salami, peppers, onions and whatever else Mr. Fanelli was serving up. Even in a snowstorm, Fanelli found the time to satisfy his customers.

DeVontray turned the corner and walked toward the back of the store. With the **exception** of him and a few snow covered trash cans, the alley was completely empty. He looked to the right, then walked closer to the three trash cans behind *Fanelli's*. They would be the only trash cans that held food in this alley. The other cans were filled with office paper, bags of dirty coffee cups and empty video tape cases. Spreading his legs as he walked, he took his time walking closer to the cans. He couldn't fall now.

Even though DeVontray didn't see anyone nor hear anything, he couldn't be too sure no one or nothing was there. One night he had walked up to the cans and was surprised by an unfriendly cat. Another night, a very old man and his wife were digging through the trash cans, placing all the food they'd found in a big garbage bag.

The closer DeVontray came to the trash cans, the better he was able to see the tip of a box peeping from underneath the lid of the can. He lifted the lid and found exactly what it was he was wishing for. A wide pizza box. Opening the pizza box, he could see that someone had only eaten one slice out of an entire pepperoni and sausage pizza! Underneath the box of pizza was a bag of food. DeVontray ripped open the bag. A plastic container of chicken popped open and red sauce dripped through his fingers. He licked his fingers, one by one.

Mmmmm.

There were long, short and fat bread rolls in the trash. Bits of lettuce, tomatoes and carrots fell out of the bag. A box of spaghetti and meatballs would have spilled had DeVontray not caught them just in time.

Thank you God. Thank you so much God. DeVontray knew he wasn't going to run anywhere now. He had to go back home, wake up the boys. They'd all be feasting for days in this snowstorm. Breakfast, lunch and dinner.   This meal would be better to them than Christmas. It would be better than any fried chicken Big Red had ever brought over. It would be just great. He could think of only one problem; getting all the food home. That was something he hadn't thought of. DeVontray peeled off a slice of the cold pizza and bit

into it. He closed his eyes. Even cold, *Fanelli's* pizza was
wonderful. Just wonderful.

The more he thought about getting the rest of the food home
to his brothers, the more he chomped down on one slice of pizza after
the other, after the other, after the other, until…

He hadn't even seen the car drive up behind him. And he
certainly hadn't heard it. But he was sure he recognized the voice.

"DeVontray? Lord honey, is that you?"

His mouth was so stuffed with pizza crust, he couldn't
respond to Mrs. Green. She was sitting on the passenger's side of the
car, facing him. Mr. Green, her husband, was driving the car.

"Hey sugar," she said sweetly. "We were just coming out of
Fanelli's and turned the car around. I thought I saw somebody
moving, but..." She frowned. "You hungry?" She nodded toward the
trash can. "You're not eating any of that are you?"

DeVontray swallowed the clump of food, grabbed the pizza
box and took off down the alley. He heard **muffled** footsteps.

"Hey there!" But, the alley was a dead end. There were only
so many more steps he could take. He knew he had to surrender.
Besides, he knew he could never outrun Mr. Green in the snow. He

probably couldn't outrun him in warm weather either. His legs were just too weak, too achy and too tired.

"Hey there Lil Man," called Mr. Green. He ran in front of DeVontray and stopped. "Whatcha gone do?" he asked, placing his baseball mitt sized hands on DeVontray's shoulders.

He looked back at the car, at Mr. Green. The door was opened wide. Walking toward him with her arms outstretched was Mrs. Green. DeVontray thought of running pass the two of them. He thought of climbing on top of the building. He thought of yelling, but neither of those thoughts seemed to make much sense to him. He felt dizzy and didn't know what else to do, which way to run.

"Sweetie," Mrs. Green smiled. "We've got food back at the house." She shook her head. "So much food, you could never eat it all. You don't have to ever do this." She lifted her chin, "Now where's your momma?"

DeVontray thought about telling Mrs. Green that he hadn't seen his mother in several days. He thought about telling all of his mother's personal business, but remained silent.

"Well how is Vivian? Is she doing alright?"

Again DeVontray kept quiet about his mother, about the matches, the small glass tube. Everything.

"Look," Mrs. Green glanced toward her car and pointed, "We can take you back to our house, and you and your brothers can have a slumber party tonight, a little sleep over. Wouldn't you like that? We'll microwave some popcorn. We'll fry up some burgers. We'll feed you real good, then you can go back home first thing in the morning if you want to. We won't keep you. But tonight," she pleaded, "why don't you all just come on home with us? O.k.?"

DeVontray thought about Mrs. Green's words. He knew the Greens had a warm house, good food, popcorn and other good things uppity black folk had to eat. He thought about the arthritis in his legs and hands and how his body would ache and cramp more than ever, if he slept inside his cold house tonight. Looking up at the two of them, then over at the trash can he opened his mouth.

"My little brothers. I need to take some food home for Marquis and Keon."

Mrs. Green shook her head. DeVontray could see tears shining in her eyes. "Yes Puddin', but not like this, darling. Not ever like this." She brushed her hand over the side of his face. "You don't ever have to get food for your brothers from the trash darling."

She slid the box of pizza from his hands. "Not now, not ever. Ok?"

He felt the pat from Mr. Green's hand on his back. "Come on son. Let's get in the car. It's too cold out here for all of this."

Chapter Four

Words to Know

Advice – (noun) an opinion or suggestion about what someone should do

Convinced – (verb) to cause someone to believe that something is true

Exception – (noun) someone or something that is different from others

Certainly – (adjective) without doubt; of course

Muffled – (verb) to make a sound quieter

Chapter Four

Crossword Puzzle

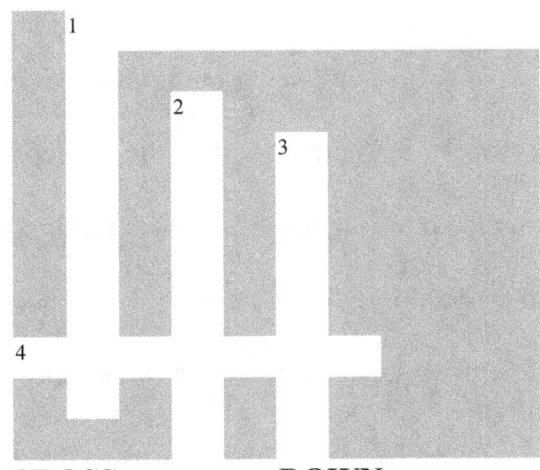

ACROSS

1. without doubt; of course
4. an opinion or suggestion about what someone should do

DOWN

1. to cause someone to believe that something is true
2. someone or something that is different from others
3. to make a sound quieter

Chapter Five

GREENER GRASS

The smell of coffee and the **chirping** of good morning birds near the window woke DeVontray from his hard sleep. All three boys had slept in the Green's guest bedroom. And just as Mrs. Green had promised, they had more food than they'd ever been able to eat. Hot dogs, burgers, fries, salad, popcorn, brownies and all the lemonade they could drink.

The breakfast table was crammed with all types of goodies. Fluffy golden eggs lay beside layers and layers of syrupy pancakes. Butter melted in the center of grits so hot, they smoked; while sausage nearly rolled off the sides of their crowded plates. Small glasses of orange juice and milk washed down every morsel of food. And not even a crisp of bacon was found anywhere on the three boys' plates. They'd eaten it all.

"You children have lovely **appetites**," said Mrs. Green.

"They sure do," Mr. Green smiled, clinking the coffee spoon onto the saucer. To DeVontray, it seemed that Mr. and Mrs. Green were happier than they were, sitting around their kitchen table.

Although he was grateful to the Greens for all they had done, DeVontray suspected that their visit would, at some point, come to an end. Even if he had an idea of what to say, he wasn't exactly sure how to ask the Greens what it was he was thinking.

"Boys," Mr. Green said after eating, "we have to talk." He reached for a toothpick.

DeVontray shrugged then shook his head. "Are you kicking us out? And if you are, when do you want us to leave?"

"Do we have to?" Keon asked.

"Yes," DeVontray answered flatly.

Marquis dropped his bottom lip, "I want my mommy now," he whispered. His crying went from a teeny tiny **whimper** to yelling so loud, DeVontray was sure everyone in the neighborhood could hear his baby brother.

"I want my mommy. I want my mommy."

"Come here," DeVontray reached for his brother, but Marquis just sat in the chair crying, his forehead banging against the kitchen table.

"Now, now sugar dumpling." Mrs. Green picked up Marquis and sat him in her lap, rocking him. "See," she smiled at the other two, "we had twin boys. They're away in college now and they're not so little. But whew," she shook her head, "when they were little they would cry, cry and cry some more when Mr. Green and I left them. Remember that Waymon?"

Mr. Green twirled the toothpick in his mouth and nodded.

Marquis finally stopped crying. He rested his head on Mrs. Green's chest and closed his eyes.

"Just like **magic**," she smiled, winking at her husband.

Mr. Green looked across the table at her and smiled.

"What was it you wanted to say to us Mr. Green?" DeVontray asked.

Pulling the tooth pick from his mouth, Mr. Green picked up the spoon and stirred the coffee in his cup. He looked up from the table and stared at each of the boys. "I have some good news and I have some bad news."

"What's the good news?" shouted Keon.

DeVontray felt a sharp pain in his stomach and he wondered what Mr. Green would say.

"Yes," Mr. Green nodded. "The good news is that beginning today; you all will get a chance to have someone take really good care of you, in a very special way."

So far DeVontray was satisfied with what he'd heard. But at the same time, he was confused that there was bad news.

He stared directly into Mr. Green's eyes then frowned. "What's the bad news, then?"

Mr. Green nodded. "As much as we'd like to have you guys stay with us a little while longer, that won't be possible after today."

"Y'all are kicking us out already?"

"It's not that we're kicking you out son," Mr. Green frowned. "We..."

"Hey man, why did y'all trick us like this? Why did y'all bring us over to your house, give us all this good food, ask us all of these questions about our mommy, then tell us we can't stay here? Mommy told us not to trust y'all. She told us y'all were some uppity black folk. Now you're talking all this good news, bad news stuff.

Last night y'all told us we could stay here until our mother came back. Now today it's this junk."

Mr. Green shook his head. "We didn't trick you son." He leaned into DeVontray. "When we talked to you boys last night, we thought we were saying all the right things," he hunched his shoulders, "but this morning we made a few telephone calls, just to be on the safe side. And the people we talked to told us that Mrs. Green and I could end up in a lot of hot water if we kept you any longer than today, without telling anyone you're here." He ran his hand over his face and **exhaled**. "It's really for your own good, son. Really it is."

DeVontray sat up straight in his chair. He was upset. He felt like running away again, and never stop running this time. When would this ever end? Which adults could he ever believe? Running away would probably solve all his problems. But he knew running away now, would only mean him and his brothers being split up probably for good. DeVontray balled his hands into tiny knots, he felt like punching the table, but he thought of his brothers and rested them in his lap.

"Boys we'd love for you to stay with us forever, but…we're sure someone else can do a much better job," said Mrs. Green, "and I'm sure…"

Right away DeVontray stopped listening to her. He had to think of a new plan. A better plan. Big Red would know how to help them. But somehow he believed that even a helping hand from Big Red wouldn't be the best idea, after all.

"Will mommy come with us," Marquis looked up into Mrs. Green's eyes.

"I don't think so," Mr. Green said.

"We'll yes, maybe. Maybe she will. We'll just have to see about some things." She smiled down at Marquis and kissed his forehead. "She might precious," said Mrs. Green in a very soothing manner. "She just might."

Marquis leaned back into Mrs. Green and sighed.

"What kind of things are we going to have to see about," Keon blurted.

Chapter Five

Words to Know

Chirping - (verb) to make a short high-pitched sound

Appetites – (noun) a physical desire for food, or for liking something

Whimper – (verb) to make a quiet crying sound

Magic – (noun) a power that allows people to do impossible things

Exhaled – (verb) to breathe out

Chapter Five
Crossword Puzzle

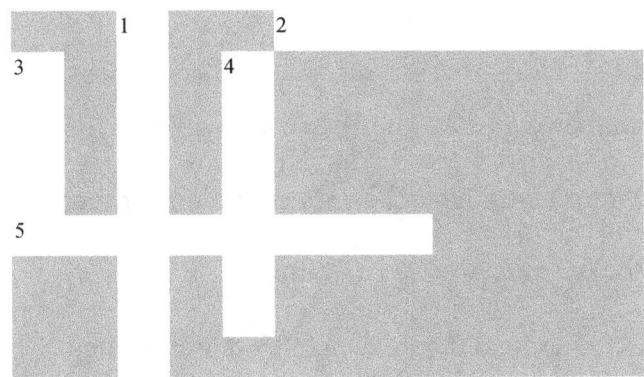

ACROSS

2. to breathe out
5. to make a short high-pitched sound

DOWN

1. a physical desire for food, or for liking something
3. a power that allows people to do impossible things
4. to make a quiet crying sound

Chapter Six

SURPRISES

In all the years DeVontray had known Mrs. Green he had never known for her to have the **expression** on her face that she had now. She looked very worried and **uneasy**.

Looking around the kitchen, DeVontray shifted in his chair. The windows in the Green's house were covered with curtains that had pretty pink and green flowery designs sewn in them. No matches or glass tubes were anywhere near those windowsills. A television sat on the kitchen counter, in the living room, another in the guest bedroom. He would even bet that there were television sets upstairs too. And there was furniture and books everywhere. Thick brown leather covered large sofas and chairs in the living room, even on the dining room chairs where they sat. And there were all kinds of tables. Some tables held more books and magazines. Others held bowls of fruit and vases with flowers almost as tall as him. It smelled nice in there too, DeVontray thought. It smelled warm, the same way his house used to smell, before his mother met Smooth. The thought of leaving all of these nice things made DeVontray sorry. If she had any extra room, DeVontray would have crawled in Mrs. Green's lap and cried just like Marquis had.

"Some people will be coming here in a few minutes," she said.

"Huh?" DeVontray frowned at Mrs. Green. "What people?"

Mrs. Green explained to the boys that a couple of nice folks were on their way to place them in another home, so that they could go live with another family for a few days, until they were able to locate their mother.

Keon and Marquis looked at DeVontray and frowned. DeVontray looked back at them, then hung his head, realizing he had let his brothers down. The reality of what Mr. Green had explained to them, was settling in quicker than he thought it would.

DeVontray **scolded** himself. If he hadn't gone out last night to look for food they would all still be at home, waiting for their mother to return. If he had just stayed inside and kept his mother's business away from the Greens, they'd be safe at home now. All three of them would be outside playing with the other neighborhood children. He shouldn't have waited so late to go to *Fanelli's* last night. He should have left right after his brothers had eaten their dinner. The Greens never would have seen him then. The **secret** about their mother being gone for days would never have been known, and the three of them wouldn't be getting ready to head over to someone else's house. If only he had waited a little longer for their mother to come home. Another five or six days, who knew? But sooner or later, she would have come home to them.

But, he thought, they had been waiting too long as it was. And if their mother was coming; she would have been home by now. Right? He bit his top lip.

The snow had stopped falling. The weather man was calling for more snow, but DeVontray felt his mother still could have come home by now if she wanted to. He wished he had stayed curled in a ball on the kitchen floor last night, **shivering**, underneath the cold oven door. He wished his mother had never quit her job, then met Smooth and made all of their furniture and heat disappear. He wished his daddy and grandma hadn't died. He wished he knew which side of town his kindergarten teacher, Ms. Wooten lived. She would understand and let them stay with her for a few days, the same as she had done, when she invited the entire kindergarten class over her house, for a weekend sleep-over. She would do it again; at least until his mother came back, DeVontray was sure of it.

"Guys," Mrs. Green shook her head, "we are so very sorry. We had no idea that your mother had been away from you for so long. It was just yesterday, when we saw her walking into the house and…"

"And the furniture," Mr. Green's face turned sour. "If your mother comes b-…"

Mr. Green was interrupted by a knock at the front door. He gave the boys a long sad look, then walked toward the door.

"Good morning," he smiled, "come on in."

Chapter Six

Words to Know

Expression – (noun) making your thoughts, feelings known by speech, writing or some other method

Uneasy – (adjective) worried or unhappy about something

Scolded – (verb) to speak in an angry way

Shivering – (verb) trembling because of cold weather

Secret – (noun) a piece of information that is hidden from other people

Chapter Six

Crossword Puzzle

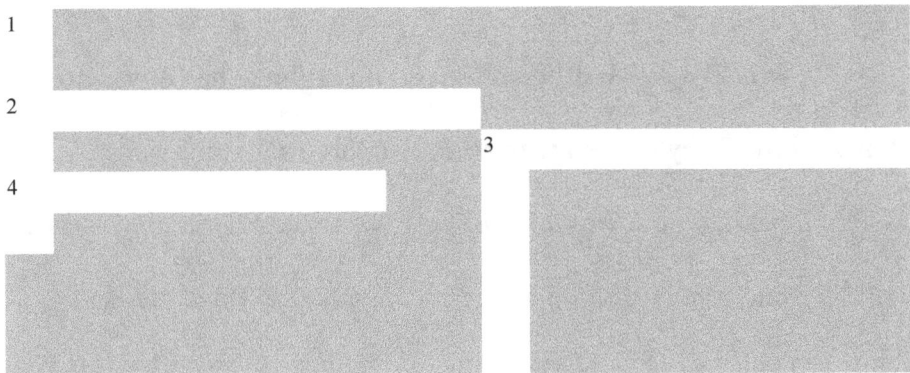

DOWN
1. worried or unhappy about something
3. a piece of information that is hidden from other people

ACROSS
2. making your thoughts, feelings known by speech, writing or some other method
3. trembling because of cold weather
4. to speak in an angry way

Chapter Seven

LOOKING BACK

Two lady police officers walked through the hallway, into the living room. They carried with them two large shopping bags. Walking behind them was another lady, who said her name was Ms. Hill. Behind Ms. Hill stood a short man with very thick glasses.

"Hello, I'm Mr. Nathan, your social worker." He **extended** his hand to DeVontray. DeVontray held his hands behind his back and stared at the man, **glaring** at him from his feet to his head. Then he turned to focus his attention on the police ladies.

Opening the shopping bags, the police ladies pulled out three very thick coats.

"Are those coats for us?" DeVontray felt excitement beating his chest.

"Thought you all would be needing these this winter," one of the police ladies said, smiling at them. From the other bag, the other police lady pulled out several shiny toy animals, cars and action figures.

"Wow," Marquis yelled.

"Oh cool." Keon smiled, "this is just like Christmas."

Marquis jumped down from Mrs. Green's lap. "Uh-uh, this is better than Christmas. Let me see," He looked at the toys his brothers held in their hands and laughed. "Sweeeeeeeet."

"We're here to help you boys," Ms. Hill said, pulling off her red leather gloves and **squatting** to look into their eyes. "We're your social workers."

She told the boys they'd soon be taken to a very sweet woman's house. Her name was Mrs. Stokes. There they'd live for a few days until their mother was found. Their new home would be called a foster home. And their new mother would be called a foster mother.

"But why can't we stay here?" DeVontray resisted.

"Mr. and Mrs. Green are not foster parents," said the police officer very calmly.

"But why can't they be our foster parents?" asked Keon, frowning.

"Yeah," Marquis chimed in, walking toward Mrs. Green, and spinning the wheel on his new car.

"Well…" Mr. Green looked at his wife and smiled, "we would make pretty lousy foster parents. We're too busy going here and there. We're always working and traveling. It wouldn't be fair to you guys," he said. "We're hardly ever at home."

"Not everyone's good at being foster parents," Ms. Hill said, patting Keon on his head.

"Why not?" asked Keon. "They were good at making us dinner and breakfast and at keeping us warm and at staying with us all night. That's being a good foster parent. So why can't they be our foster parents?"

The adults in the room chuckled.

"It's not that simple dear," said Ms. Hill.

Mr. and Mrs. Green looked at one another

"Now," Mr. Nathan cleared his throat and folded his arms, "DeMontay…"

"DeVontray," he scolded the man. "My name is DeVontray, not no DeMontay."

"Oh sure," Mr. Nathan shoved his hands in his pockets. "DeVontray," He pulled out a small square of paper and unfolded it in his hand. "O.k. DeVontray you must be the oldest. You all may ride with Ms. Hill and my-"

"Can I call my **lawyer**?" DeVontray asked Mr. Green, as he took a seat on the sofa, "'cause something doesn't seem too right. I don't want to leave here until I talk to my lawyer."

Keon ran to sit on the sofa with his brother. "Yeah, what if our mommy comes back and she won't even know where to find us?"

"Can I go with mommy?" Marquis asked, grabbing hold of Mrs. Green's hand.

"Listen," Mr. Green squatted before the boys. "My wife and I are not going to steer you guys wrong. But if you stay here with us, we'll all get in big, big trouble. And you'll never be able to visit with us again."

"Well can we just stay here for one more day?" DeVontray crossed his arms over his chest. "Why do we have to go anywhere with these weird looking people?"

Mr. Nathan sat beside DeVontray. He pushed his glasses up his nose and inhaled before speaking. The man explained to

DeVontray that he and his brothers would remain together until their mother was found.

"Just a couple of weeks at the most," Ms. Hill smiled, "and you boys should be back at home," she snapped her fingers, "just like that."

"Will they feed us at our new foster home?" Keon asked. "Will it be warm over there, like it is in here?"

"Sure it will be," Ms. Hill chuckled.

"If you're not getting enough food and heat, you call me." The police lady with the pinned up hair reached inside her shirt pocket and pulled out a card. "I'll make sure you get more than enough food and heat. O.k. buddy?" She handed the card to DeVontray.

Glancing over the card, he smiled a little on the inside, knowing he and his brothers would be warm, fed and taken care of until their mother came for them.

Teary eyed, the Greens hugged the boys. The children thanked the Greens, zipping up their new thick coats as they headed for the door. Riding out of his neighborhood, DeVontray looked back at his house.

"Stop!!!"

"What?" yelled a surprised Ms. Hill as she brought the car to an abrupt halt.

DeVontray looked at Ms. Hill through the rearview mirror and frowned. "I- I was just wondering if, well… If our mother came back last night while we were gone, she wouldn't kn-"

"Now listen…"

"I mean, she may think we're just outside playing and she might get worried and come looking for us and…"

"Yeah, can we see if mommy got home yet?" Keon asked.

Mr. Nathan shook his head and looked at Ms. Hill. "I don't think it's a good idea Kalikwa. I mean if she's not there, this whole thing could get really ugly and…"

"Can I just go run in there and see though?" DeVontray stared at Ms. Hill through the rearview mirror. "Pleeeaase, just this one time? Pretty please?"

Ms. Hill closed her eyes. "O.k.," she whispered. "Just this once." She opened her eyes.

The other boys crawled out of the car behind their brother, but Ms. Hill called for them to come back.

"Let him see if your mom's in the house first."

Running through his front yard in the snow, DeVontray climbed the stairs to the door and knocked. He walked toward the window. No curtains hung there. Cupping his hands over his eyes, he peeped inside. The inside of his house had not changed since last night. Covers lay on the hardwood floor, but still there was no furniture. Only the stool beside the window. DeVontray knocked again. In just that instant he thought he saw his mother scurry behind the refrigerator. He blinked, then looked again. He couldn't be too sure, but he was almost **positive** he'd just seen his mother. Hadn't he? Was he just imagining, hoping for her to be there? No. She's there. Right there behind the refrigerator.

"Mommy?" DeVontray called, "it's me mommy, Vonnie." He knocked and knocked and knocked again. Over and over, hoping his mother would move from behind the refrigerator and open the door.

"Mommy are you in there? It's me Vonnie." He brushed the snow from his fluffy jacket. "Look," he extended his arms, "a brand new coat." His mother would like his new coat. He knew she would. Again he knocked. And again his knocks went unanswered. There was no movement in their house. Although the rest of his body was cold, his knuckles began warming up from all the knocking and banging. Regardless of how badly his hands hurt, he would knock all day and night if he had to, until his mother opened the door. Those weird people, the social workers, The Greens, and everyone else would know his mommy was still a good mommy. She loved him. She loved his brothers. She wasn't bad like he knew they believed she was.

"Mommy. It's Von-"

"DeVontray?"

He spun in a half circle to see Ms. Hill standing behind him. Disappointed, he exhaled.

"She's not in there sweetie," she said, cold air seeping from her mouth.

"But, I just saw her in there Ms. Hill. She's right behind the refrig-"

"No darling," she looked through the window. "No honey. She's not there."

"She's there. I know I saw her. I'm not blind."

Ms. Hill shook her head and wrapped her arms around his shoulders.

Burying his head into Ms. Hill's chest, DeVontray did something he hadn't done in a very long time.

He cried.

Chapter Seven

Words to Know

Extended – (verb) to cause something to straighten out or to stretch out

Glaring – (verb) to look directly at someone in an angry way

Squatting – (verb) to bend your knees and lower your body so that you are close to your heels or sitting on your heels

Lawyer – (noun) a person whose job is to guide and assist people in matters relating to the law

Positive – (adjective) thinking about the good qualities of someone or something

Chapter Seven

Crossword Puzzle

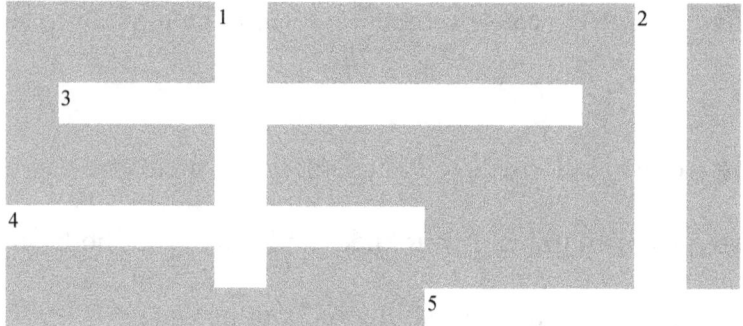

ACROSS

3. to bend your knees and lower your body so that you are close to your heels or sitting on your heels
4. to cause something to straighten out or to stretch out
5. a person whose job is to guide and assist people in matters relating to the law

DOWN

1. to look directly at someone in an angry way
2. thinking about the good qualities of someone or something

Chapter Eight

MOVING ON

The little house on Lemon Street smelled like a restaurant with all types of **delicious aromas** seeping through it.

"Hello there," Mrs. Stokes chirped, delighted to meet the boys. The short, chubby woman clapped her hands and giggled, flipping a piece of peppermint candy on her tongue.

"My oh my, oh my," she exclaimed," three cute, little boys. Harold would have loved to be around to see all of you. Yes indeedy." She clapped her hands again and hugged each of the boys, as if she hadn't seen them in years. From behind the sofa, a dog barked. DeVontray jumped at the sudden noise.

"Oh don't worry about him Love," Mrs. Stokes said, "that's Dog. He's just old and feeble minded. I wouldn't doubt if he's not many years older than me already. He's not going to do any more than you ask him. Too old," she **giggled**. "He'll just lay there behind the sofa for the rest of the day and look like a bump on a log. Nice company though. Good to have around. You all will probably have to drag him, if you want him to go outside and play with you."

She brushed the front of her apron. "Now, my Harold is no longer with us." She pointed at the picture on the table of a tall man in a wide hat. "But, when my Harold was in the land of the living, he and I were presented a **certificate** by the mayor of this city. We were so active in this neighborhood with all the children, and all. Those children are all grown and gone now, but I tell you, we really enjoyed our time with them. Planning lots of activities, taking them here, taking them there." She went to the wall and pulled the certificate from it. "Good times back then," she chuckled, "very good times." With the sleeve of her sweater, Mrs. Stokes wiped off the certificate.

"*Citizenship of Excellence Awarded to Harold and Glodene Stokes...,*" she read. "See, read it for yourself." She passed the shiny piece of wood over to Mr. Nathan.

"This is very nice ma'am," he said. "I don't doubt you one bit."

Ms. Hill smiled at the boys. "You all are in very good hands, here."

The older lady placed her hand on Ms. Hill's shoulder. "You don't have to worry none about me knowing how to take care of anybody else's children sugar. No, ma'am. Not one little bit," she shook her head. "I've been taking care of children for years and years and years and years and years and years." She put her hands on her hips and looked at both Ms. Hill and Mr. Nathan," I guess all those children are around you alls ages now." She laughed. "That's how long it's been. Harold and I weren't able to have any children of our very own, you see. I'm a retired school teacher and I loved taking care of children back then, and I love it now. **Absolutely** love it."

Mrs. Stokes turned and walked toward the kitchen. "Come on let's eat before the food gets cold." Stopping to face everyone she said, "I may as well let you all know right now. I'm from a little town in South Carolina. And you know we down home folk can whip up some good cooking. And I mean some good cooking too. And we don't like to see any good food setting around getting cold neither. We'll leave all that cold for outdoors," she laughed while walking into the kitchen.

That night as DeVontray lay on the top bunk of the bed, the night light on, he thought about all that had happened to him and his brothers in just one day. He wondered whether his mother had gotten home by now. He couldn't help but wonder whether or not she had come from behind the refrigerator. Something told him that it was her he had seen. But he slowly began **dismissing** that thought, realizing that if his mother had been in the house, she would have opened the door for him.

So far Mrs. Stokes seemed to be a very sweet lady. She kept them laughing as she made up songs for them to sing. She had even taught them a few card games. And before she went to bed, she invited them to join her in some yoga exercises. DeVontray smiled, remembering how the three of them had giggled at the older lady getting down on the floor stretching her legs, bending her arms and arching her back. Mrs. Stokes was just too funny; DeVontray smiled to himself and thought of how she reminded him of his grandmother, who'd died last year.

Finally he thought of their new friend, Dog. Not only had Dog been good company for Mrs. Stokes, he'd also been lots of fun for them to have around. Every since they'd gotten familiar with him, they had kept Dog busy running with them in the snow, jogging after sticks they'd thrown to him, eating dog biscuits and bathing.

They had taken such a liking to Dog that Mrs. Stokes told them that as long as they could stand his company, Dog would be allowed to sleep in the same room with them. Propping himself on his elbows, DeVontray peeped over at Dog, as he lay snoring on the floor, next to Marquis' bed. DeVontray lay back on his bed and imagined the day he'd be able to show Dog to their mother.

Right then he made a decision.

Chapter Eight

Words to Know

Delicious – (adjective) a very pleasant taste

Aromas – (noun) a noticeable and usually pleasant smell

Certificate – (noun) a document that is proof that something has happened

Absolutely – (adjective) with no limitation

Dismissing – (verb) to decide not to think about or consider something or someone

Chapter Eight
Crossword Puzzle

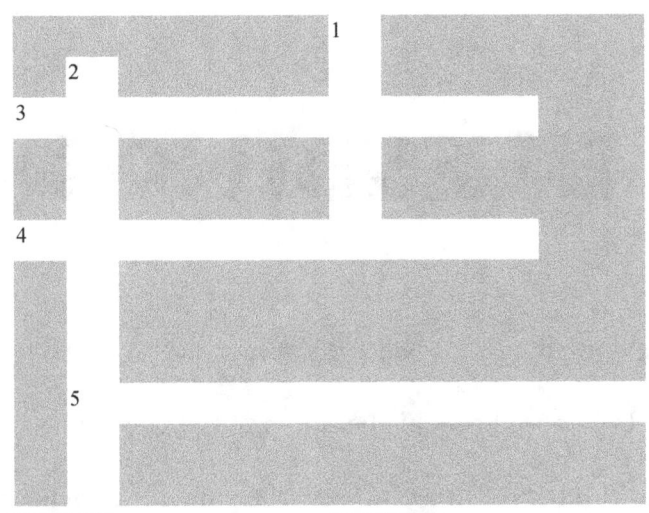

ACROSS

3. a very pleasant taste
4. to decide not to think about or consider something or someone
5. with no limitation

DOWN

1. a noticeable and usually pleasant smell
2. a document that is proof that something has happened

Chapter Nine

COUNTING

BLESSINGS

Crawling out of his bed, DeVontray slid from the top bunk of the bed, to the floor. From his bedroom to the kitchen he stumbled through the darkness. Tip-toeing pass the sofa, the television set and end tables, DeVontray reached the kitchen then stopped; listening to make sure no one had followed him in the darkness. Confident he was alone; he lifted the telephone from the wall and dialed. If his mother was sleeping, his phone call would wake her. If she was still living and walking around Richmond, Virginia, he would do everything in his power to find her and bring her back to them. He would even **introduce** her to Mrs. Stokes and his case workers. He'd also tell her how the Greens were not uppity like she always said they were.

By the fifty-sixth ring, he realized she either wasn't home or had no plans of answering the telephone. As if in a daze, DeVontray slid the telephone from his ear and placed it back on its cradle. Pulling himself from the wall, he walked over to the trash can and kicked it.

"Is everything alright?"

DeVontray heard Mrs. Stokes behind him, but did not look her way. **Unable** to control his anger, he extended his leg then kicked the wall. First his right foot, then his left.

"Where," he karate chopped the wall, "are you?"

"Now baby, that wall is pretty tough. It's been standing in the same place for decades. But if you keep kicking it like that, I doubt your feet will be able to stand for much longer than a minute."

Ignoring Mrs. Stokes' words, DeVontray did not turn. Instead, he kicked again and again.

"Well," she said heading over to the kitchen counter, "I may as well make myself a big pot of coffee and watch this show up close." She yawned and **shuffled** her slippered feet toward the coffee pot. "I can tell this is going to be a very, very long night. But keep going," she waved to him, "don't mind me. And by all means, don't let me stop you."

Out of the corner of his eye, DeVontray watched Mrs. Stokes roll up the sleeves of her nightgown as she walked past him, humming. She was right; she wasn't going to stop him. And the more he kicked, the more he hurt himself. The burning pain started in his feet and traveled up the back of his legs. He knew the kicking wasn't good for his arthritis, because all over his body he was beginning to feel pain. If he didn't stop he would be kicking the wall all night long and still he wouldn't have put a dent, a whole nor a crack in the wall as he had been able to do at school.

As if she wasn't a bit bothered by DeVontray's tantrum, Mrs. Stokes pulled down a cup and saucer from the cabinet and stopped humming. "How you like yours? With or without cream?"

"Huh?" He lost his balance and stumbled forward.

"Your coffee, baby. With or without cream?"

"I don't..."

"Well you obviously need a cup of coffee if whatever you're going through is treating you that bad. Now what will it be? With cream or without?"

He felt his face scrunch into a ball. "But, I…"

"Anyone feeling so bad they have to go around kicking and punching things really needs a hot cup of something to warm themselves up. Don't you think?" Reaching up into the cabinet, Mrs. Stokes set out another cup and saucer. From a drawer she pulled out some spoons. "I understand you being upset about a few changes in your life, but you can't allow other people to cause you to hurt yourself, no matter who they are."

As much as he didn't want to admit it, this crazy old woman was beginning to make a lot of sense.

"You want me to whip you up something to eat?" she asked.

"No, thank you."

"Well if you don't want anything to eat and you don't want any coffee, here's a cup of hot cocoa coming up," she grabbed a large jug of milk from the refrigerator, and shook it. "Now I'm sure you can think of so many things to be thankful for." Pouring the milk into a small pot with one hand, she rested the other hand on her hip and **sighed**. "So why don't you start counting?"

"Ma'am?"

"Count your blessings." She looked over her glasses at him and walked to the microwave to heat the cocoa. "I know you have more blessings than you can think. You can't even count them all. Now can you?"

DeVontray shook his head. Already he was beginning to feel a little calmer. He stared at her. This wasn't the way the teachers treated him when he threw **tantrums** in front of everyone at school. Mrs. Stokes wasn't screaming at him, nor was she calling him names that made him feel bad about himself. She was calm the same way his mother used to be, before daddy and Gramma Nanny passed away. DeVontray wasn't sure what Mrs. Stokes was up to, but he knew he didn't want her leaving him there in the kitchen all alone. With her, he felt safe and somehow relieved that she wasn't so in a hurry to leave him standing by himself to think things through.

Chapter Nine

Words to Know

Introduce – (verb) to cause something to be used for the first time

Unable – (adjective) not able to do something

Shuffled – (verb) to slide your feet along the ground or back and forth without lifting them completely

Sighed – (verb) to take in and let out a long, loud breath in a way that shows you are bored, disappointed or relieved

Tantrums – (noun) an uncontrolled expression of childish anger

Chapter Nine

Crossword Puzzle

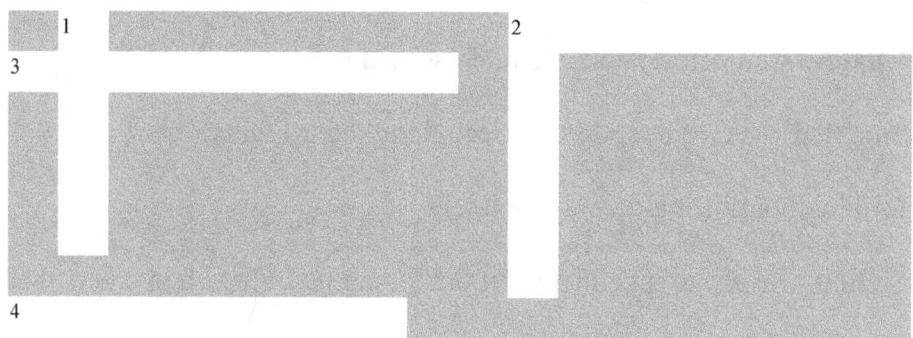

ACROSS

2. to slide your feet along the ground or back and

forth without lifting them completely
3. to cause something to be used for the first time
4. an uncontrolled expression of childish anger

DOWN

1. not able to do something

2. to take in and let out a long, loud breath in

a way that shows you are bored, disappointed

or relieved

Chapter Ten

FRIENDLY

FACES

"Good Lordy I'm tired," she said, taking the cocoa out of the microwave and setting both cups of beverage on the table. "Honey, you have your good health. You're living inside a nice warm house. You have two brothers living here with you; who think the world of you. And for goodness sake," she slid his hot cocoa closer to him, "you have plenty of good **common sense**. Now what more can you ask for?"

"My mommy." Like melted butter, the words poured from his mouth into the stillness of the kitchen. It was too late to grab them, put them in his mouth and swallow. They had already been spoken. **Embarrassed**, he lowered his head.

Mrs. Stokes nodded. "Sit down here a minute son." She pulled out a chair and patted the back of it. "Right here."

Careful with his steps, DeVontray inched his way toward the table, sitting across from Mrs. Stokes. Although the words were quick to spill from his lips, he was surprised by his **honesty** toward this woman, this stranger.

"Tell me all about it."

Looking into the older woman's eyes, he was reminded of his Gramma Nanny, and of how much he really did miss her. Like Gramma Nanny, Mrs. Stokes gave DeVontray the feeling that she knew everything. He also had the feeling that she had all the answers to his questions, before he could even ask them. Deep behind those eyes was tenderness, kindness, joy and a love so strong it warmed him better than any cup of cocoa ever could. Mrs. Stokes seemed as if she really wanted to listen to his **troubles**. And in spite of what his mother would have said, he told them to her. Every single one of them.

"You are my son. You and your brothers. You're my sons," she said smiling after listening to all he'd said, "the good Lord sent you to me. And as long as He keeps me here on this earth, I'm going to treat you just like you all are my very own children. Do you understand me?"

"Yes ma'am."

"Sugar, there's one thing that you're going to have to know about this life," she **paused**, "it never ever matters where you start. The only thing that really matters in this life is how you finish."

She clasped her hands over his, bowed her head, then closed her eyes. "Let's go before the good Lord in prayer."

Chapter Ten

Words to Know

Common Sense – (noun) the ability to think and behave in a reasonable way and to make good decisions

Embarrassed – (verb) to make someone feel confused or foolish

Honesty – (noun) being fair and truthful

Paused – (verb) to stop doing something for a short time before doing it again

Troubles – (noun) problems or difficulties

Chapter Ten

Crossword Puzzle

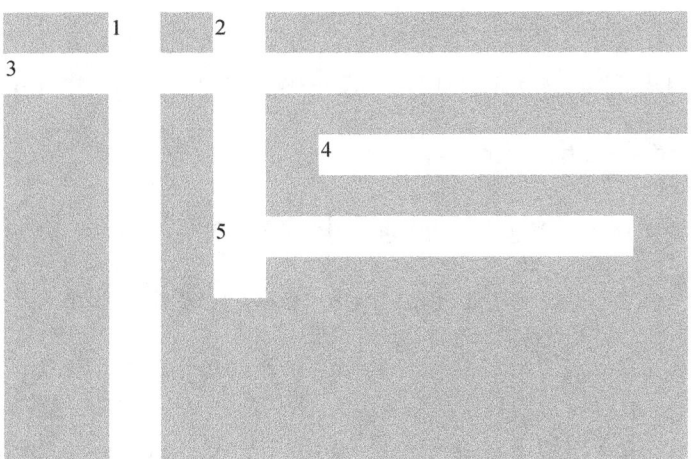

ACROSS

3. the ability to think and behave in a reasonable way and to make good decisions
4. to stop doing something for a short time before doing it again
5. problems or difficulties

DOWN

1. to make someone feel confused or foolish
2. being fair and truthful

Chapter Eleven

LIFE'S LESSONS

Faster than a go kart rolling down an icy hill, an entire year had sped by without anyone really noticing. Although, the boys and Mrs. Stokes had patiently waited, no word came from, nor about their mother. The **social worker** Mr. Nathan constantly called, checking in on DeVontray and his brothers. And Ms. Hill, who attended their church, stopped by most Sundays for Mrs. Stokes' mouthwatering dinners.

Their new neighborhood was quieter, with fewer children, but they all enjoyed one another's company. None of their new friends attended school with them. Their new school was different. At school, children were introduced to **Swahili**, Spanish, sign language, algebra and the history of the kings and queens of Africa. Even though they were given twice as much homework than they'd ever had, learning had become a fun and rewarding **experience** for them.

Once a month Mrs. Stokes paid for the boys to remain in school. And once a month they brought home report cards filled mostly with E's, for excellent. At first DeVontray and his brothers thought their new school was horrible. There were only fifty students in the entire school. It was too small. Even the food in the cafeteria was strange. Lots of crunchy vegetables, fruits of all kinds and dishes that included mostly, lamb, chicken, turkey and fish.

Weird.

DeVontray's new life had turned out to be much different than he ever imagined. Although he missed his mother, Mrs. Stokes made sure their bodies and minds were constantly occupied. They helped rebuild Dog's house, constructed a basketball hoop, planted seeds in Mrs. Stokes vegetable garden, made greeting cards for the sick and shut in at church and repaired Mr. Stokes' "coo-coo" clock.

On Saturday mornings they pulled out their swimming trunks and towels and headed over to the YMCA, where they took lessons. Mrs. Stokes swam at the other end of the pool with the adults. Later in the day, Mr. and Mrs. Green would come by to take the boys downtown to Mukhtaar's School of Drama. There the children learned how to speak in front of large groups, write colorful paragraphs and pretend they were make – believe people. Mr. Mukhtaar called these make - believe people, characters. Although swimming helped improve the pains DeVontray suffered from his arthritis, drama helped him develop a relationship with people he never ever thought possible. He was able to **imagine** that he was someone else. Living in other places; wherever his imagination took him, he was there.

Drama gave DeVontray the confidence he needed to stand up before a group of people and recite long sentences. For the first time in a long time, no one laughed at or made fun of him when he spoke, not even the teacher. Instead, they applauded him and cheered him on to speak more. Devontray was very interested in this whole new world of drama and creating make - believe characters. When Mr. Mukhtaar asked the class to develop characters for the upcoming play, he not only thought of a character for himself, but he was also able to help other students develop their characters as well. The drama teacher was so impressed with him; he decided to give DeVontray the lead character in the upcoming play.

The play was about a family who had moved down from New York to Virginia. The adjustments the children in the family made to their new surroundings were the highlights of the play. Each

of the drama students expressed themselves in many ways. Some

danced, some sang, others played musical instruments. But all of the

students had a chance to speak as a make-believe character.

By the time Friday, the day of the play had come around,

DeVontray could hardly sit still. At the breakfast table he

couldn't stop talking about the big night.

"Not so fast there son," Mrs. Stokes beamed, as she wiped up

the milk DeVontray

had spilled on the table, while aiming for the cereal bowl.

"DeVontray's making a big mess," Keon laughed.

"Well he's just being a little nervous about tonight." Mrs.

Stokes rubbed Keon's cheeks, "that's all. He's just a big bundle of

nerves right now."

"I wonder how many people are going to be there tonight?"

Devontray asked smiling at his brothers.

"This many," Marquis stretched his arms as wide as they'd

go.

"Remember sweetie," Mrs. Stokes looked over her glasses at

Marquis, "we don't talk with food in our mouths."

"I bet everyone in Richmond is going to be there tonight," said Keon. "DeVontray already told everybody in the school and they told their friends, and they told their friends, and they told their friends and…"

"Alright," Mrs. Stokes chuckled, "let's not get too carried away. Besides all of Richmond could never fit inside of your drama school."

"Mrs. Stokes?" DeVontray looked up at her.

"Yes Puddin'?"

"What if I forget my lines? I mean what if I forget everything we've been practicing all this time and I get out there and can't remember a thing. What if that huh?"

She folded her arms. "Now if all of that happens tonight, you just bow your head, close your little eyes and ask the good Lord above to help you remember every word that He has placed in that big, smart brain of yours." She rubbed his head.

"That's right DeVontray," Keon chimed in.

Chapter Eleven

Words to Know

Social Worker - (noun) a person who helps people with social work

Swahili – (noun) a language widely used in East Africa and the Congo region

Experience – (noun) the process of doing and seeing things happen to you

Weird – (noun) something unbelievable; unnatural

Imagine – (verb) to form a picture or create something that is not real, in your mind

Chapter Eleven

Crossword Puzzle

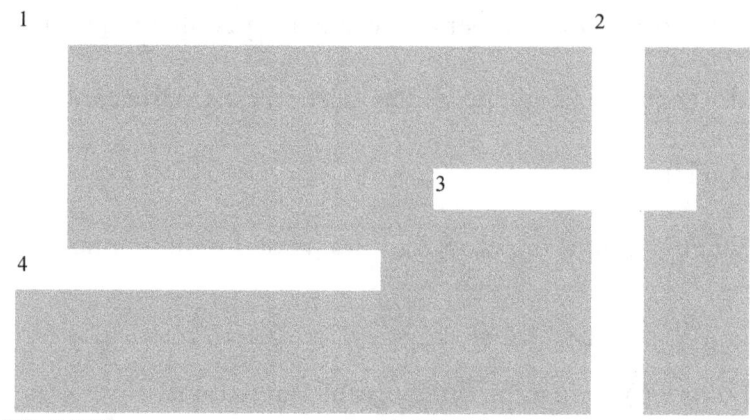

ACROSS

1. a person who helps people with social work
3. something unbelievable; unnatural
4. to form a picture or create something that is not real, in your mind

DOWN

1. a language widely used in East Africa and the Congo region
2. the process of doing and seeing things happen to you

Chapter Twelve

DRAMA KINGS

Throughout the day in school, DeVontray watched the clock. When he wasn't counting the hours before show time, he was rehearsing his lines over and over in his mind. He even had two of his friends listen to him repeat the lines at recess.

"Man if you keep this up, you're going to be just like Terrance Howard," said one of his friends.

"Or like Tyler Perry," said the other.

DeVontray listened to his friends and thought of all the great people Mr. Mukhtaar had taught them about during **drama** class. He imagined acting on the big, big stages of the world, just like Ira Aldridge, Paul Robeson and Lawrence Fishburne. He wondered whether or not he would ever get up the nerve to star in movies as Moses Gunn, Ossie Davis and Denzel Washington had. Finally, he imagined himself writing about **characters** and directing actors behind a movie camera.

"Could I?" he asked himself.

He heard Mr. Mukhtaar's words over and over in his head. "If you work hard, you can be anything you want to be. Nothing and no one can stop a made up mind."

Right then DeVontray knew, he too could make movies like Oscar Micheaux, Melvin Van Peebles and Spike Lee.

"Hey," he said to himself, "one day, I am going to be anything I want to be." His new confidence put a brand new pep in his step.

Immediately after school, the boys ate their snacks, completed their homework and prepared to head down to the drama school.

Peeping from behind the curtain, DeVontray could see that there were so many people in the audience. There were two van loads of senior citizens and a bus from Mrs. Stokes' church. There were so many people walking in to see the play; it had to start twenty – five minutes late.

Behind stage, Mr. Mukhtaar and all of the **performers** joined hands in a circle. The chant was led by their drama teacher.

"Repeat after me please," said Mr. Mukhtaar. "All that is good and accomplished in the world takes work. Everything else. Everything else. Everything else. Is jive."

The performers repeated the teacher's words. One by one they squeezed each other's hands before dropping them to their sides.

"Let's go give these people the best show they've ever seen. I know you can do it. I believe in each and every one of you. You're all destined for greatness. So now," he looked at each one of them. "Let God have His way in you tonight. O.k?"

"O.k.," they chimed in clapping for one another.

Throughout the performance DeVontray felt as if he were floating in the clouds. He remembered all of his lines; spoke them with so much meaning and enthusiasm that many people in the audience laughed at things, he hadn't even thought were funny. At the end of the show's performance, the actors took their bows, as the audience stood, cheering wildly for their outstanding performance.

Mr. Mukhtaar walked onstage. "Let's give our youth another round of applause," he swept his hand over the cast of actors. "And feel free to come up shake their hands. Congratulate them on their performances tonight."

So many people came up to the stage shaking the children's hands, patting their backs and **encouraging** them. Joining them were the social workers, Mr. Nathan and Ms. Hill and the two lady police officers they'd met a year ago at Mr. and Mrs. Green's house.

"Wow," Marquis yelled, "you guys came too?"

"Sure we came too. Thought we wouldn't?"

"You guys were absolutely **terrific**," said Mr. Nathan.

Ms. Hill put her hands on her hips, "DeVontray how'd you manage to learn all of those lines?"

"Practice makes perfect," he laughed, pushing out his chest.

Chapter Twelve

Words to Know

Characters – (noun) the way someone thinks, feels and behaves

Drama – (noun) writing that tells a story and is performed on a stage

Performance – (noun) an activity that a person or a group does to entertain an audience

Terrific – (adjective) extremely good; causing a feeling of surprise or wonder

Encouraging – (verb) to make someone more determined, hopeful, or confident

Chapter Twelve

Crossword Puzzle

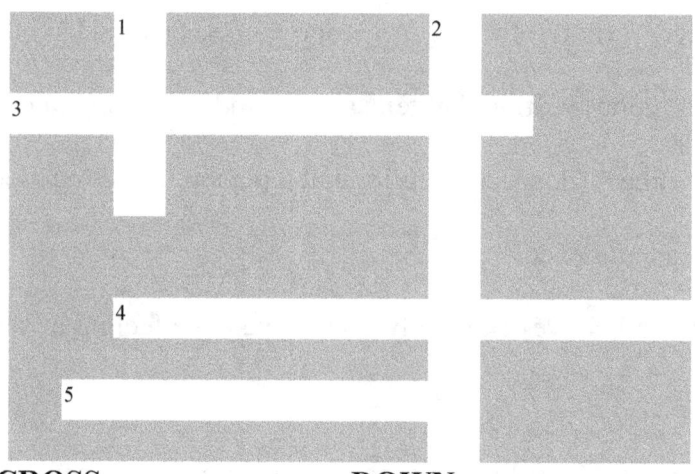

ACROSS

DOWN

3. the way someone thinks, feels and behaves
4. to make someone more determined, hopeful, or confident
5. extremely good; causing a feeling of surprise or wonder

1. writing that tells a story and is performed on a stage
2. an activity that a person or a group does to entertain an audience

Chapter Thirteen

WELCOME HOME

Mrs. Stokes waited behind stage to greet the boys. "I knew you all could do it," she said, hugging them. "I knew you could. I just knew you could. **Praise** the good Lord."

Bringing a large bouquet of flowers were Mr. and Mrs. Green. "Well, well look at the three actors," Mrs. Green pulled out bunches of flowers for all three of the boys.

"I know boys don't generally **prefer** flowers, but now that you all are big time actors, I just thought that you'd probably want these."

The boys laughed. "Thank you," they said.

"Well," Mr. Green said, reaching in his back pocket, "Mrs. Green brought you flowers, but I thought you might like something a little more…well a little more…"

"What is it?" asked Keon.

"Should I tell them?" he asked winking at Mrs. Green.

"Yes," Keon said, "tell us."

Mrs. Green nodded. "Why not?"

Mr. Green tilted his head and smiled at the boys. "Well gentlemen, Mrs. Green and I are on our way to see a tiny little mouse who just so happens to live way down in Florida. And we just wanted to know if you guys wanted to come along with us."

"A mouse?" Marquis asked. "I don't even like mouses."

"Mice," Keon corrected him. "There's no such thing as mouses."

Mr. Green held up a handful of tickets. "I don't know if you guys have ever heard of him, but this little mouse's name is Mickey."

"Ever hear of him?" asked Mrs. Green.

"Mickey the Mouse?" Marquis asked.

"Down in Florida?" asked DeVontray.

"Are those tickets to see the Disney World Mickey Mouse?" Keon shouted, "all the way in Disney World, in Florida?"

"You bet," said Mrs. Green.

The boy's eyes widened with joy, as they jumped up and down.

"I can't believe it. We're going to Disney World?" DeVontray shouted. "Oh yes. Sweet."

Keon reached up to give DeVontray a high five. "When do we leave?" he asked.

"As soon as you all can get your clothes packed. You all can spend the rest of the evening with us, and as soon as you wake up in the morning we're out of here first thing." Mrs. Green smiled. "Our plane leaves very early in the morning."

"A plane?" Marquis clapped. "Oh man!!!"

On the way home the boys chatted endlessly about their trip. They were so excited they ran all the way from the car to the front door of the house.

"We need our coats in Florida."

"No we don't Keon," Marquis squealed, "Mr. Green said it's going to be real hot in Florida."

"Fellas," Mrs. Stokes called for them, as they took off upstairs to their bedroom. "Come back down a moment please."

Running back down the stairs, nearly tripping over one another, they stood in the living room. Dog stood between them barking.

"Yes?"

"I've already packed your suitcases. You don't have to worry about getting any more clothes together." She unbuttoned her coat and rested it on the coat rack. "But I do have something very important, I'd like to discuss with you all right now."

"Now?" Marquis frowned.

"Yes sir."

"Aren't you coming to Disney World with us Mrs. Stokes?" DeVontray asked. "Did you pack your things too?"

"No son," she opened her purse and pulled out some papers. "This is a trip Mr. and Mrs. Green have been preparing for you all for quite some time now. It's their gift to the three of you."

"Is something wrong then Mrs. Stokes?" Keon asked, his shoulders **slouching**.

"No my darling," she scratched the side of her face, "everything's just as right as right can be."

Unfolding the papers, she sat in her favorite chair and looked up at each of them. "These papers came today. I didn't know how or when to tell you all, so I decided to do it after your performance tonight and not a moment later."

DeVontray felt that old knot forming in his stomach again. All of a sudden he knew something was wrong. "What is it then?"

"Children, these papers are called **adoption** papers." She smoothed the papers over her lap. "It's been more than a year, and still no one has been able to find your mother. But I decided the very day I laid my eyes on the three of you, that I would use every dime I had, to give each of you the most beautiful home possible. And God willing, I am going to continue doing just that. I feel like you all are my very own children, the children I never had." She smiled. "And from now on, I am your mother." She patted her lap. "These papers say so. You're not my foster children and I am not your foster mother. Not anymore. Whatever you need, whenever you need it, I'll be right there to provide it for you. There'll be no more money coming from the state to help feed you and clothe you. Uh - uh. From now on, whatever I have is yours."

"Just like that?" DeVontray asked.

"Just like that," Mrs. Stokes smiled. "My husband Harold left me a nice chunk of money before he died. And I'm going to use it to see that each of my boys goes all the way to **college** and even to the White House if you want to. Is that alright?"

"That's alright," Marquis smiled, exposing gums, where two front teeth should have been.

"Yes," Keon replied, "that's just fine."

DeVontray thought of his mother, Smooth, Big Red and everyone else he hadn't seen in a year. He remembered the prayer he prayed that night before Mr. and Mrs. Green had found him in the alley behind *Fanelli's* and he looked up, knowing that God had given him his brand new world. God had answered his prayers in His own special way.

"Yes Mrs. Stokes. It's alright," DeVontray felt the smile spread over his face and the knot dissolve in his stomach. He and his brothers would be safe and happy from now on. He walked to the couch hugging their new mother.

"Yes," he said, "Praise the Lord. This is alright."

Chapter Thirteen

Words to Know

Praise – (verb) to say good things about someone

Generally – (adverb) in a way that is not detailed or specific

Slouching – (verb) to walk, sit or stand lazily with your head and shoulders bent forward

Adoption – (noun) the act of parents bringing home a child to live with them

College – (noun) a school students attend after finishing high school

Chapter Thirteen
Crossword Puzzle

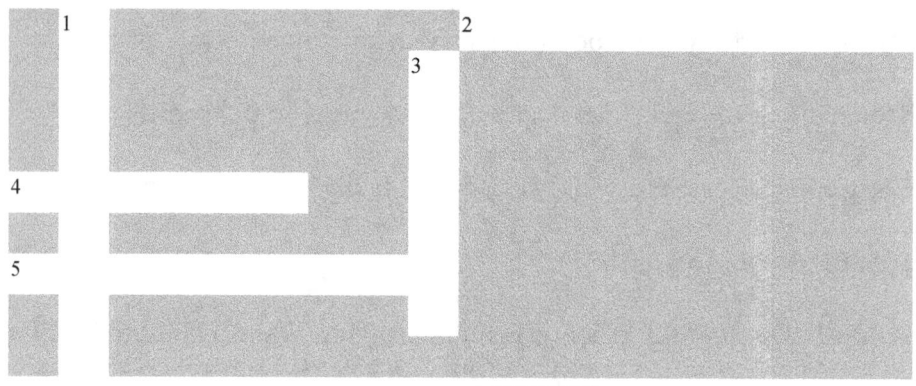

ACROSS

3. he act of parents bringing home a child to live with them
4. to say good things about someone
5. to walk, sit or stand lazily with your head and shoulders bent forward

DOWN

1. in a way that is not detailed or specific
3. a school students attend after finishing high school

Chapter One

Fill In The Blank

1. Everything had been in the middle of the_____ floor, just as it always had been.

(a). Living room

(b.) Kitchen

(c.) Bedroom

(d). Dining Room

2. Pouring a glass of _____into the large frying pan, he opened the bag of dried noodles and crushed them into the pan.

(a.) water

(b.) juice

(c.) milk

(d.) coffee

3. "Where are we supposed to _____ down?" Marquis asked.

(a.) lie

(b.) sit

(c.) fall

(d.)go

Chapter Two

Fill In The Blank

1. The more he wiped his round face, the faster the _____

   rolled.

   (a.) tears

   (b.) sweat

   (c.) wheels

   (d.) toys

2. Man, how he wished he had prayed harder to God about

   keeping the _____ away.

   (a.) rain

   (b.) snow

   (c.) hurricane

   (d.) thunderstorm

3. DeVontray knew how to _____.

   (a.) drive

   (b.) sew

   (c.) cook

(d.)clean

Chapter Three

Fill In The Blank

1. If he acted out at _____, there would be other people to calm him back down.

   (a.) church

   (b.) home

   (c.) school

   (d.) work

2. Their mother worked her job at the _____, came home and cooked delicious hot food for them to eat.

   (a.) church

   (b.) school

   (c.) restaurant

   (d.) post office

3. Dear: Keon and Marquis, I have to go find _____.

   (a.) Smooth

   (b.) mommy

   (c.) granny

(d.) daddy

Chapter Four

Fill In The Blank

1. Other than to find food, _____ had no idea where he was going.

   (a.) DeVontray

   (b.) Marquis

   (c.) Keon

   (d.) Smooth

2. One night he had walked up to the cans and was surprised by an unfriendly _____.

   (a.) dog

   (b.) cat

   (c.) monkey

   (d.) squirrel

3. "Come on son. Let's get in the car. It's too _____ out here for all of this."

   (a.) windy

   (b.) hot

   (c.) cold

(d.) rainy

Chapter Five
Fill In The Blank

1. Hot dogs, burgers, fries, salad, popcorn, brownies and all the
   lemonade they could _____.

   (a.) eat

   (b.) drink

   (c.) take

   (d.) hold

2. "Boys," Mr. Green said after eating, "we have to talk." He
   reached for a _____.

   (a.) pickle

   (b.) napkin

   (c.) fork

   (d.) toothpick

3. "Will mommy come with us," _____ looked up into Mrs.
   Green's eyes.

   (a.) Marquis

   (b.) Smooth

(c.) DeVontray

(d.) Mr. Green

Chapter Six

Fill In The Blank

1. If she had any extra room, _____ would have crawled

   in Mrs. Green's lap and cried just like Marquis had.

   (a.) DeVontray

   (b.) Marquis

   (c.) Keon

   (d.) Smooth

2. He wished his _____ and _____hadn't died.

   (a.) daddy and grandma

   (b.) mommy and grandpa

   (c.) aunt and uncle

   (d.) teacher and principal

3. _____ was interrupted by a knock at the front door.

   He gave the boys a long sad look, then walked toward the

   door.

   (a.) DeVontray

   (b.) Keon

(c.) Mr. Green

(d.) Mrs. Green

Chapter Seven

Fill In The Blank

1. Marquis jumped down from Mrs. Green's lap. "Uh-uh, this is

better than _____.

    (a). Valentine's Day

    (b.) Easter

    (c.) Thanksgiving

    (d.) Christmas

2. "But why can't they be our _____?" asked Keon, frowning.

(a.) neighbors

(b.) teachers

(c.) foster parents

(d.) friends

3. Burying his head into Ms. Hill's chest, DeVontray did something

he hadn't done in a very long time.

    He _____.

    (a.) laughed

(b.) smiled

(c.) cried

(d.) frowned

Chapter Eight

Fill In The Blank

1. The little house on _____ smelled like a

   restaurant with all types of **delicious** aromas seeping

   through it.

   (a.) Lemon Street

   (b.) Apple Street

   (c.) Strawberry Street

   (d.) Banana Street

2. _____ turned and walked toward the kitchen.

   "Come on let's eat before the food gets cold."

   (a.) Mr. Green

   (b.) Mrs. Green

   (c.) Mrs. Stokes

   (d.) Mr. Nathan

3. Every since they'd gotten familiar with him, they had kept

   _____ busy running with them in the snow, jogging

after sticks they'd thrown to him, eating dog biscuits and

bathing.

(a.) Dog

(b.) Cat

(c.) Pet

(d.) Owl

Chapter Nine

Fill In The Blank

1. Pulling himself from the wall, he walked over to the trash can

   and _____ it.

   (a.) hugged

   (b.) hit

   (c.) threw

   (d.) kicked

2. Reaching up into the cabinet, Mrs. Stokes set out another

   _____ and _____.

   (a.) cup and saucer

   (b.) fork and spoon

   (c.) shoe and sock

   (d.) bread and butter

3. "Count your _____." She looked over her glasses at him

   and walked to the microwave to heat the cocoa.

   (a.) blessings

   (b.) eggs

(c.) forks

(d.) thoughts

Chapter Ten

Fill In The Blank

1. Looking into the older woman's eyes, he was reminded of his

   _____, and of how much he really did miss her.

   (a.) teacher

   (b.) mommy

   (c.) Grandma Nanny

   (d.) Papa

2. "You are my _____. You and your brothers. You're

   my sons," she said smiling after listening to all he'd said, "the

   good Lord sent you to me.

   (a.) daughter

   (b.) student

   (c.) neighbor

   (d.) son

3. She clasped her hands over his, bowed her head, then closed

   her eyes. "Let's go before the good _____ in prayer."

   (a.) Lord

(b.) Man

(c.) Preacher

(d.) Master

Chapter Eleven

Fill In The Blank

1. Faster than a _____ rolling down an icy hill, an entire

    year had sped by without anyone really noticing.

    (a.) rollercoaster

    (b.) motorcycle

    (c.) go kart

    (d.) bicycle

2. Once a month Mrs. Stokes paid for the boys to remain in

    school. And once a month they brought home report cards

    filled mostly with E's, for _____.

    (a.) Eating

    (b.) Eager

    (c.) Excellent

    (d.) Eggs

3. "Now if all of that happens tonight, you just _____ your

    head, close your little eyes and ask the good Lord above to

help you remember every word that He has placed in that big,

smart brain of yours." She rubbed his head.

(a.) close

(b.) bow

(c.) nod

(d.) lift

Chapter Twelve

Fill In The Blank

1. He heard _____ words over and over in his

   head. "If you work hard, you can be anything you want to be.

   Nothing and no one can stop a made up mind."

   (a.) Mr. Mukhtaar's

   (b.) Mommy's

   (c.) Mr. Green's

   (d.) Mr. Nathan's

2. The performers repeated the teacher's words. One by one

   they squeezed each other's _____ before dropping them to

   their sides.

   (a.) shoulders

   (b.) toes

   (c.) hands

   (d.) feet

3. "Practice makes _____," he laughed, pushing out his chest.

   (a.) great

(b.) excellent

(c.) cakes

(d.) perfect

Chapter Thirteen
Fill In The Blank

1. Mrs. Stokes waited behind stage to greet the boys. "I knew

   you all could do it," she said, hugging them. "I knew you

   could. I just knew you could. _____the good Lord."

   (a.) Praise

   (b.) Wave

   (c.) Smile

   (d.) Shout

2. "Well gentlemen, Mrs. Green and I are on our way to see a

   tiny little _____ who just so happens to live way down in

   Florida.

   (a.) mouse

   (b.) dog

   (c.) cat

   (d.) owl

3. And I'm going to use it to see that each of my boys goes all

the way to **college** and even to the _____ if you want to.

Is that alright? "Neighbor

(a.) Green House

(b.) Brown House

(c.) Red House

(d.) White House

Word Find

S	N	O	W	N
D	O	G	O	A
O	A	M	Q	C
R	E	E	I	T
L	U	N	C	H

Word Find Vocabulary

Snow

Lemon

Dog

Lunch

Act

Him

Character Related Discussion Questions

1. Describe your favorite character(s) throughout the book.

2. What makes the character (s) your favorite?

3. Who in real life reminds you of the character(s)? Why?

4. If you could change one thing about your favorite character(s), what would it be?

5. Who is your least favorite character? Why?

Complete The Story

1. What happens after the brothers return from Walt Disney World with the Greens?

2. Will the boys ever become reunited with their mother? If so, explain.

3. How should Mr. and Mrs. Green continue their relationship with the boys?

4. Should the boys remain at the school or return to their old school with their old and familiar friends?

5. If you were a friend of the boys, to whom would you be closest?

6. Describe the life of each of the boys once they've grown up. What career paths do you think they will choose?

The End